50 STATES
TRAVEL CHALLENGE

CHALLENGE YOURSELF TO VISIT ALL 50 U.S. STATES
(and washington d.c.)

Other Titles in The "Challenge Books" Series:

Everyone's A Critic - 52 Week Movie Challenge
Everyone's A Critic - 52 Week Movie Challenge - Horror Edition
Everyone's A Critic - 52 Week Book Challenge
Everyone's A Food Critic - 52 Week Restaurant Challenge

wandering tortoise

© 2019, 2023 Patricia N. Hicks.
All rights reserved.

No part of this publication may be reproduced, distributed or transmitted
in any form or by any means, including photocopying, recording,
or other electronic or mechanical methods, without prior
written permission of the author, except as permitted by U.S. copyright law.

ISBN: 978-1695862197

U.S. STATES TRAVEL CHALLENGE
Visit All The States To Complete The Challenge

☐ Alabama   ☐ Alaska   ☐ Arizona   ☐ Arkansas

☐ California   ☐ Colorado   ☐ Connecticut   ☐ Delaware

☐ Florida   ☐ Georgia   ☐ Hawaii   ☐ Idaho

☐ Illinois   ☐ Indiana   ☐ Iowa   ☐ Kansas

☐ Kentucky   ☐ Louisiana   ☐ Maine   ☐ Maryland

U.S. STATES TRAVEL CHALLENGE
Visit All The States To Complete The Challenge

- [ ] Massachusetts
- [ ] Michigan
- [ ] Minnesota
- [ ] Mississippi

- [ ] Missouri
- [ ] Montana
- [ ] Nebraska
- [ ] Nevada

- [ ] New Hampshire
- [ ] New Jersey
- [ ] New Mexico
- [ ] New York

- [ ] North Carolina
- [ ] North Dakota
- [ ] Ohio
- [ ] Oklahoma

- [ ] Oregon
- [ ] Pennsylvania
- [ ] Rhode Island
- [ ] South Carolina

U.S. STATES TRAVEL CHALLENGE
Visit All The States To Complete The Challenge

☐ South Dakota ☐ Tennessee ☐ Texas ☐ Utah

☐ Vermont ☐ Virginia ☐ Washington ☐ West Virginia

☐ Wisconsin ☐ Wyoming ☐ Washington, DC

ALABAMA

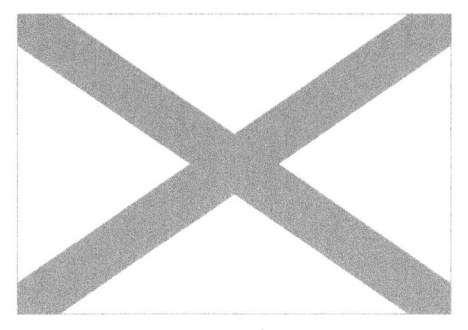

State Flag

Admission To Statehood: December 14, 1819 (The 22nd State)
Nickname: Yellowhammer State   **Capital City:** Montgomery
State Motto: Audemus jura nostra defendere (We Dare Maintain Our Rights)
State Bird: Yellowhammer   **State Tree:** Longleaf Pine
State Flower: Camellia   **State Song:** "Alabama"

Date(s) visited:

Who did you travel with?

How did you get there (car, plane, train, etc.):

Place(s) you stayed (hotel, campground, etc.):

☆☆☆☆☆
☆☆☆☆☆
☆☆☆☆☆

Place(s) you visited (landmarks, parks, festivals, points of interest):

☆☆☆☆☆
☆☆☆☆☆
☆☆☆☆☆
☆☆☆☆☆
☆☆☆☆☆
☆☆☆☆☆

What was your favorite place to visit? Why?

Places you ate (restaurants, family's home, etc.):

☆☆☆☆☆

☆☆☆☆☆

☆☆☆☆☆

☆☆☆☆☆

☆☆☆☆☆

What local food specialties did you try?

What things do you want to do or see the next time you visit?

DID YOU KNOW? The first electric streetcar system was debuted in Montgomery, Alabama on April 15, 1886. It was nicknamed "Lightning Route". 119 years later, "Lightning Route," is re-introduced as a G.P.S. guided trolley system, the first in the nation, with audio tours of the city's historic sites.

ALASKA

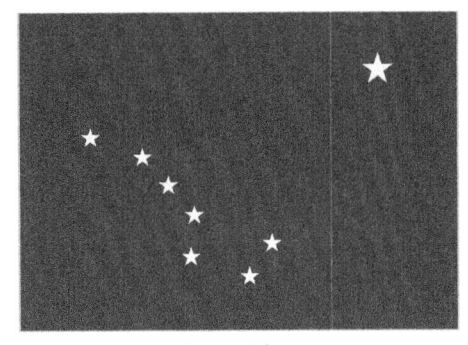

State Flag

Admission To Statehood: January 3, 1959 (The 49th State)
Nickname: The Last Frontier   **Capital City:** Juneau
State Motto: North To The Future
State Bird: Willow Ptarmigan   **State Tree:** Sitka Spruce
State Flower: Forget-Me-Not   **State Song:** "Alaska's Flag"

Date(s) visited: _____

Who did you travel with? _____

How did you get there (car, plane, train, etc.): _____

Place(s) you stayed (hotel, campground, etc.):

Place(s) you visited (landmarks, parks, festivals, points of interest):

What was your favorite place to visit? Why?

Places you ate (restaurants, family's home, etc.):

☆☆☆☆☆
☆☆☆☆☆
☆☆☆☆☆
☆☆☆☆☆
☆☆☆☆☆

What local food specialties did you try?

What things do you want to do or see the next time you visit?

DID YOU KNOW? Aurora borealis (the northern lights) are produced by charged electrons and protons striking the earth's upper atmosphere. They can be seen in Fairbanks an average of 4 out of 5 nights from August 21st to April 21st when the sky is dark and clear.

ARIZONA

State Flag

Admission To Statehood: February 14, 1912 (The 48th State)
Nickname: The Grand Canyon State   **Capital City:** Phoenix
State Motto: Ditat Deus (God enriches)
State Bird: Cactus Wren   **State Tree:** Palo Verde
State Flower: Saguaro Cactus Blossom   **State Song:** "Arizona"

Date(s) visited:

Who did you travel with?

How did you get there (car, plane, train, etc.):

Place(s) you stayed (hotel, campground, etc.):

☆☆☆☆☆

☆☆☆☆☆

☆☆☆☆☆

Place(s) you visited (landmarks, parks, festivals, points of interest):

☆☆☆☆☆

☆☆☆☆☆

☆☆☆☆☆

☆☆☆☆☆

☆☆☆☆☆

☆☆☆☆☆

What was your favorite place to visit? Why?

Places you ate (restaurants, family's home, etc.):

☆☆☆☆☆
☆☆☆☆☆
☆☆☆☆☆
☆☆☆☆☆
☆☆☆☆☆

What local food specialties did you try?

What things do you want to do or see the next time you visit?

DID YOU KNOW? London Bridge, which was built in 1831 over the Thames River in London, England, was dismantled and brought to Arizona in 1968 where it was rebuilt in Lake Havasu City.

ARKANSAS

State Flag

Admission To Statehood: June 15, 1836 (The 25th State)
Nickname: The Natural State **Capital City:** Little Rock
State Motto: Regnat populus (The people rule)
State Bird: Northern Mockingbird **State Tree:** Loblolly Pine
State Flower: Apple Blossom **State Song:** "Arkansas"

Date(s) visited:

Who did you travel with?

How did you get there (car, plane, train, etc.):

Place(s) you stayed (hotel, campground, etc.):

☆☆☆☆☆

☆☆☆☆☆

☆☆☆☆☆

Place(s) you visited (landmarks, parks, festivals, points of interest):

☆☆☆☆☆

☆☆☆☆☆

☆☆☆☆☆

☆☆☆☆☆

☆☆☆☆☆

☆☆☆☆☆

What was your favorite place to visit? Why?

Places you ate (restaurants, family's home, etc.):

☆☆☆☆☆
☆☆☆☆☆
☆☆☆☆☆
☆☆☆☆☆
☆☆☆☆☆

What local food specialties did you try?

What things do you want to do or see the next time you visit?

DID YOU KNOW? Mountain View is a small community deep in the Ozark mountains. Established in the 1870s, this "Folk Music Capitol of the World", is dedicated to preserving the traditional music and "folkways" (way of life) of the area.

CALIFORNIA

State Flag

Admission To Statehood: September 9, 1850 (The 31st State)
Nickname: Golden State   **Capital City:** Sacramento
State Motto: Eureka (I have found it)
State Bird: California Quail   **State Tree:** California Redwood
State Flower: California Poppy **State Song:** "I Love You, California"

Date(s) visited:

Who did you travel with?

How did you get there (car, plane, train, etc.):

Place(s) you stayed (hotel, campground, etc.):

☆☆☆☆☆

☆☆☆☆☆

☆☆☆☆☆

Place(s) you visited (landmarks, parks, festivals, points of interest):

☆☆☆☆☆

☆☆☆☆☆

☆☆☆☆☆

☆☆☆☆☆

☆☆☆☆☆

☆☆☆☆☆

What was your favorite place to visit? Why?

Places you ate (restaurants, family's home, etc.):

☆☆☆☆☆
☆☆☆☆☆
☆☆☆☆☆
☆☆☆☆☆
☆☆☆☆☆

What local food specialties did you try?

What things do you want to do or see the next time you visit?

DID YOU KNOW? Some of the giant redwood trees located in the Sequoia National Forest are estimated to be more than 2000 years old. The Sequoia National Park (California's first National Park) can boast having the largest living tree...its trunk circumference is 102 feet!

COLORADO

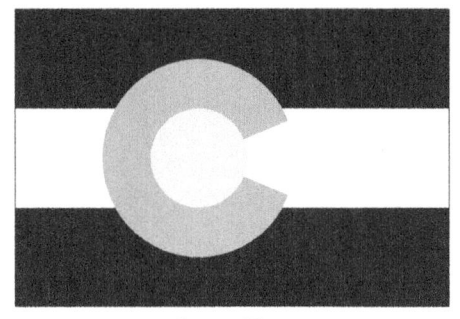

State Flag

Admission To Statehood: August 1, 1876 (The 38th State)

Nickname: Centennial State **Capital City:** Denver

State Motto: Nil Sine Numine (Nothing Without Providence)

State Bird: Lark Bunting **State Tree:** Colorado Blue Spruce

State Flower: Rocky Mountain Columbine **State Song:** "Where The Columbines Grow"

Date(s) visited:

Who did you travel with?

How did you get there (car, plane, train, etc.):

Place(s) you stayed (hotel, campground, etc.):

☆☆☆☆☆

☆☆☆☆☆

☆☆☆☆☆

Place(s) you visited (landmarks, parks, festivals, points of interest):

☆☆☆☆☆

☆☆☆☆☆

☆☆☆☆☆

☆☆☆☆☆

☆☆☆☆☆

☆☆☆☆☆

What was your favorite place to visit? Why?

Places you ate (restaurants, family's home, etc.):

☆☆☆☆☆

☆☆☆☆☆

☆☆☆☆☆

☆☆☆☆☆

☆☆☆☆☆

What local food specialties did you try?

What things do you want to do or see the next time you visit?

DID YOU KNOW? The highest paved road in North America is the Mount Evans Scenic Byway. It climbs to over 14,000 feet above sea level. Be sure to pack a jacket for a trip to Mount Evans. In the summer, the temperature there can be 50° cooler than in Denver!

CONNECTICUT

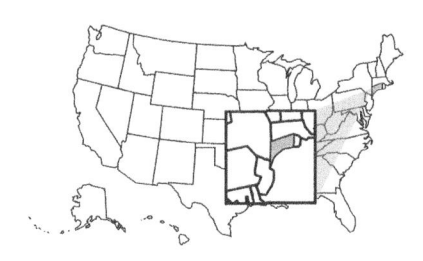

State Flag

Admission To Statehood: January 9, 1788 (The 5th State)
Nickname: Constitution State   **Capital City:** Hartford
State Motto: Qui transtulit sustinet (He who is transplanted sustains)
State Bird: American Robin   **State Tree:** White Oak
State Flower: Mountain Laurel   **State Song:** "Yankee Doodle"

Date(s) visited: _____

Who did you travel with? _____

How did you get there (car, plane, train, etc.): _____

Place(s) you stayed (hotel, campground, etc.):

_____   ☆☆☆☆☆

_____   ☆☆☆☆☆

_____   ☆☆☆☆☆

Place(s) you visited (landmarks, parks, festivals, points of interest):

_____   ☆☆☆☆☆

_____   ☆☆☆☆☆

_____   ☆☆☆☆☆

_____   ☆☆☆☆☆

_____   ☆☆☆☆☆

_____   ☆☆☆☆☆

What was your favorite place to visit? Why?

Places you ate (restaurants, family's home, etc.):

☆☆☆☆☆
☆☆☆☆☆
☆☆☆☆☆
☆☆☆☆☆
☆☆☆☆☆

What local food specialties did you try?

What things do you want to do or see the next time you visit?

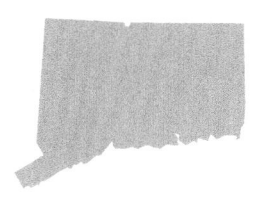

DID YOU KNOW? The Hartford Courant is the largest daily newspaper in Connecticut. Established on October 29, 1764 (before American independence), it is also often recognized as the oldest U.S. newspaper in continuous publication.

DELAWARE

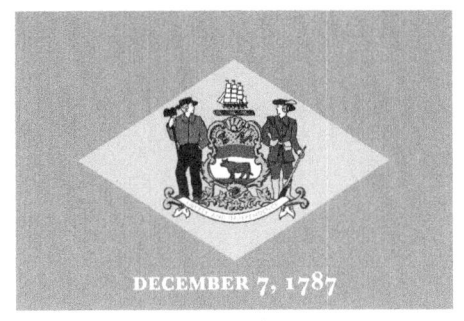

State Flag

Admission To Statehood: December 7, 1787 (The 1st State)
Nickname: First State **Capital City:** Dover
State Motto: Liberty and Independence
State Bird: Delaware Blue Hen **State Tree:** American Holly
State Flower: Peach Blossom **State Song:** "Our Delaware"

Date(s) visited:

Who did you travel with?

How did you get there (car, plane, train, etc.):

Place(s) you stayed (hotel, campground, etc.):

☆☆☆☆☆

☆☆☆☆☆

☆☆☆☆☆

Place(s) you visited (landmarks, parks, festivals, points of interest):

☆☆☆☆☆

☆☆☆☆☆

☆☆☆☆☆

☆☆☆☆☆

☆☆☆☆☆

☆☆☆☆☆

What was your favorite place to visit? Why?

Places you ate (restaurants, family's home, etc.):

☆☆☆☆☆
☆☆☆☆☆
☆☆☆☆☆
☆☆☆☆☆
☆☆☆☆☆

What local food specialties did you try?

What things do you want to do or see the next time you visit?

DID YOU KNOW? The log cabin, originating in Europe, was brought to America by Scandinavian settlers arriving in Delaware in the 1600s. In the 1800s the log cabin became a symbol of the American pioneer and it continues to enjoy that iconic status today.

FLORIDA

State Flag

Admission To Statehood: March 3, 1845 (The 27th State)
Nickname: Sunshine State   **Capital City:** Tallahassee
State Motto: In God We Trust
State Bird: Mockingbird   **State Tree:** Sabal Palm
State Flower: Orange Blossom   **State Song:** "Swanee River"

Date(s) visited:

Who did you travel with?

How did you get there (car, plane, train, etc.):

Place(s) you stayed (hotel, campground, etc.):

☆☆☆☆☆

☆☆☆☆☆

☆☆☆☆☆

Place(s) you visited (landmarks, parks, festivals, points of interest):

☆☆☆☆☆

☆☆☆☆☆

☆☆☆☆☆

☆☆☆☆☆

☆☆☆☆☆

☆☆☆☆☆

What was your favorite place to visit? Why?

_____
_____
_____

Places you ate (restaurants, family's home, etc.):

_____ ☆☆☆☆☆
_____ ☆☆☆☆☆
_____ ☆☆☆☆☆
_____ ☆☆☆☆☆
_____ ☆☆☆☆☆

What local food specialties did you try? _____
_____
_____

What things do you want to do or see the next time you visit? _____
_____
_____
_____
_____

DID YOU KNOW? Saint Augustine, Florida founded in 1565, is the country's oldest European settlement. It is home to Ponce de Leon's legendary Fountain of Youth as well as "The Oldest Wooden Schoolhouse" in the nation (circa 1716).

GEORGIA

State Flag

Admission To Statehood: January 2, 1788 (4th State)
Nickname: Peach State   **Capital City:** Atlanta
State Motto: Wisdom, Justice, Moderation
State Bird: Brown Thrasher   **State Tree:** Southern Live Oak
State Flower: Cherokee Rose   **State Song:** "Georgia On My Mind"

Date(s) visited:

Who did you travel with?

How did you get there (car, plane, train, etc.):

Place(s) you stayed (hotel, campground, etc.):

☆☆☆☆☆
☆☆☆☆☆
☆☆☆☆☆

Place(s) you visited (landmarks, parks, festivals, points of interest):

☆☆☆☆☆
☆☆☆☆☆
☆☆☆☆☆
☆☆☆☆☆
☆☆☆☆☆
☆☆☆☆☆

What was your favorite place to visit? Why?

Places you ate (restaurants, family's home, etc.):

☆☆☆☆☆

☆☆☆☆☆

☆☆☆☆☆

☆☆☆☆☆

☆☆☆☆☆

What local food specialties did you try?

What things do you want to do or see the next time you visit?

DID YOU KNOW? Approximately 200 million pounds of Vidalia Onions, known as the "sweetest onion in the world," are distributed across North America each year. The Granex onion hybrid can only earn the Vidalia name if it is grown in very specific areas of Georgia where the onions develop a much sweeter flavor.

HAWAII

State Flag

Admission To Statehood: August 21, 1959 (The 50th State)

Nickname: Aloha State   **Capital City:** Honolulu

State Motto: Ua Mau ke Ea o ka 'Āina i ka Pono (The life of the land is perpetuated in righteousness)

State Bird: Hawaiian goose (Nēnē)   **State Tree:** Candlenut Tree

State Flower: Hawaiian Hibiscus (ma'o hau hele)   **State Song:** "Hawai'i Pono'ī"

Date(s) visited:

Who did you travel with?

How did you get there (car, plane, train, etc.):

Place(s) you stayed (hotel, campground, etc.):

☆☆☆☆☆

☆☆☆☆☆

☆☆☆☆☆

Place(s) you visited (landmarks, parks, festivals, points of interest):

☆☆☆☆☆

☆☆☆☆☆

☆☆☆☆☆

☆☆☆☆☆

☆☆☆☆☆

☆☆☆☆☆

What was your favorite place to visit? Why?

Places you ate (restaurants, family's home, etc.):

☆☆☆☆☆
☆☆☆☆☆
☆☆☆☆☆
☆☆☆☆☆
☆☆☆☆☆

What local food specialties did you try?

What things do you want to do or see the next time you visit?

DID YOU KNOW? There are five active volcanoes in Hawaii ("active" meaning it has erupted within the last 10,000 years). Four of them are on Hawaii (Big Island): Kilauea, Mauna Loa, Mauna Kea, and Hualalai. The fifth, Mount Haleakala, is on Maui.

IDAHO

State Flag

Admission To Statehood: July 3 1890 (The 43rd State)

Nickname: Gem State **Capital City:** Boise

State Motto: Esto perpetua (Let It Be Perpetual)

State Bird: Mountain Bluebird **State Tree:** Western White Pine

State Flower: Syringa **State Song:** "Here We Have Idaho"

Date(s) visited:

Who did you travel with?

How did you get there (car, plane, train, etc.):

Place(s) you stayed (hotel, campground, etc.):

☆☆☆☆☆

☆☆☆☆☆

☆☆☆☆☆

Place(s) you visited (landmarks, parks, festivals, points of interest):

☆☆☆☆☆

☆☆☆☆☆

☆☆☆☆☆

☆☆☆☆☆

☆☆☆☆☆

☆☆☆☆☆

What was your favorite place to visit? Why?

Places you ate (restaurants, family's home, etc.):

☆☆☆☆☆

☆☆☆☆☆

☆☆☆☆☆

☆☆☆☆☆

☆☆☆☆☆

What local food specialties did you try?

What things do you want to do or see the next time you visit?

DID YOU KNOW? Heaven's Gate Lookout is located within the Nez Perce National Forest. From the lookout, sightseers can view the Seven Devils' Mountains, Snake River Canyon, and mountain peaks in four different states: Idaho, Montana, Oregon and Washington.

ILLINOIS

State Flag

Admission To Statehood: December 3, 1818 (The 21st State)
Nickname: Prairie State   **Capital City:** Springfield
State Motto: State Sovereignty, National Union
State Bird: Cardinal   **State Tree:** White Oak
State Flower: Purple Violet (Viola) **State Song:** "Illinois"

Date(s) visited:

Who did you travel with?

How did you get there (car, plane, train, etc.):

Place(s) you stayed (hotel, campground, etc.):

☆☆☆☆☆
☆☆☆☆☆
☆☆☆☆☆

Place(s) you visited (landmarks, parks, festivals, points of interest):

☆☆☆☆☆
☆☆☆☆☆
☆☆☆☆☆
☆☆☆☆☆
☆☆☆☆☆
☆☆☆☆☆

What was your favorite place to visit? Why?

___

Places you ate (restaurants, family's home, etc.):

___ ☆☆☆☆☆

___ ☆☆☆☆☆

___ ☆☆☆☆☆

___ ☆☆☆☆☆

___ ☆☆☆☆☆

What local food specialties did you try?

___

What things do you want to do or see the next time you visit?

___

DID YOU KNOW? The earliest versions of pizza didn't have cheese or tomatoes in the ingredient list. Thank goodness our present day pizzerias aren't sticklers for tradition! When you're visiting Illinois, be sure to to sample the iconic, cheese-loaded "Chicago-style" deep-dish pizza.

INDIANA

State Flag

Admission To Statehood: December 11, 1816 (The 19th State)

Nickname: Hoosier State **Capital City:** Indianapolis

State Motto: The Crossroads Of America

State Bird: Cardinal **State Tree:** Tulip Tree

State Flower: Peony **State Song:** "On The Banks Of The Wabash"

Date(s) visited:

Who did you travel with?

How did you get there (car, plane, train, etc.):

Place(s) you stayed (hotel, campground, etc.):

☆☆☆☆☆

☆☆☆☆☆

☆☆☆☆☆

Place(s) you visited (landmarks, parks, festivals, points of interest):

☆☆☆☆☆

☆☆☆☆☆

☆☆☆☆☆

☆☆☆☆☆

☆☆☆☆☆

☆☆☆☆☆

What was your favorite place to visit? Why?

_____

_____

_____

_____

Places you ate (restaurants, family's home, etc.):

_____	☆☆☆☆☆
_____	☆☆☆☆☆
_____	☆☆☆☆☆
_____	☆☆☆☆☆
_____	☆☆☆☆☆

What local food specialties did you try?

_____

_____

What things do you want to do or see the next time you visit?

_____

_____

_____

_____

DID YOU KNOW? Because of this small town's unusual name, the post office in Santa Claus, Indiana receives thousands of letters from around the world addressed to Santa. Since 1914, a group of volunteers called "Santa's Elves" has worked to ensure every child receives a reply.

IOWA

State Flag

Admission To Statehood: December 28, 1846 (The 29th State)
Nickname: Hawkeye State   **Capital City:** Des Moines
State Motto: Our liberties we prize and our rights we will maintain
State Bird: Eastern Goldfinch   **State Tree:** Bur Oak
State Flower: Wild Prairie Rose **State Song:** "The Song of Iowa"

Date(s) visited:

Who did you travel with?

How did you get there (car, plane, train, etc.):

Place(s) you stayed (hotel, campground, etc.):

☆☆☆☆☆

☆☆☆☆☆

☆☆☆☆☆

Place(s) you visited (landmarks, parks, festivals, points of interest):

☆☆☆☆☆

☆☆☆☆☆

☆☆☆☆☆

☆☆☆☆☆

☆☆☆☆☆

☆☆☆☆☆

What was your favorite place to visit? Why?

_____
_____
_____
_____

Places you ate (restaurants, family's home, etc.):

Place	Rating
_____	☆☆☆☆☆
_____	☆☆☆☆☆
_____	☆☆☆☆☆
_____	☆☆☆☆☆
_____	☆☆☆☆☆

What local food specialties did you try?

_____
_____
_____

What things do you want to do or see the next time you visit?

_____
_____
_____
_____
_____

DID YOU KNOW? If you happen to visit Strawberry Point, Iowa, you will find the world's largest strawberry. It's hard to miss. The 15-foot berry is actually a painted fiberglass statue of a strawberry dating back to the 1960s.

KANSAS

State Flag

Admission To Statehood: January 29, 1861 (The 34th State)
Nickname: Sunflower State   **Capital City:** Topeka
State Motto: Ad astra per aspera (To the stars through difficulties)
State Bird: Western Meadowlark   **State Tree:** Eastern Cottonwood
State Flower: Sunflower   **State Song:** "Home on the Range"

Date(s) visited:

Who did you travel with?

How did you get there (car, plane, train, etc.):

Place(s) you stayed (hotel, campground, etc.):

☆☆☆☆☆
☆☆☆☆☆
☆☆☆☆☆

Place(s) you visited (landmarks, parks, festivals, points of interest):

☆☆☆☆☆
☆☆☆☆☆
☆☆☆☆☆
☆☆☆☆☆
☆☆☆☆☆
☆☆☆☆☆

What was your favorite place to visit? Why? _____

_____

_____

_____

Places you ate (restaurants, family's home, etc.):

_____	☆☆☆☆☆
_____	☆☆☆☆☆
_____	☆☆☆☆☆
_____	☆☆☆☆☆
_____	☆☆☆☆☆

What local food specialties did you try? _____

_____

_____

What things do you want to do or see the next time you visit? _____

_____

_____

_____

_____

DID YOU KNOW? There are three types of prairie habitats and Kansas has all of them. The High Plains of western Kansas feature shortgrass prairies. The Flint Hills are the largest remaining expanse of tallgrass prairie in the world. And the Smoky Hills and Red Hills in the central portion of Kansas have a mixed habitat (both shortgrass and tallgrass).

KENTUCKY

State Flag

Admission To Statehood: June 1, 1792 (The 15th State)
Nickname: Bluegrass State   **Capital City:** Frankfort
State Motto: United We Stand, Divided We Fall
State Bird: Northern Cardinal   **State Tree:** Tulip Tree
State Flower: Goldenrod   **State Song:** "My Old Kentucky Home"

Date(s) visited: _____

Who did you travel with? _____

How did you get there (car, plane, train, etc.): _____

Place(s) you stayed (hotel, campground, etc.):

☆☆☆☆☆
☆☆☆☆☆
☆☆☆☆☆

Place(s) you visited (landmarks, parks, festivals, points of interest):

☆☆☆☆☆
☆☆☆☆☆
☆☆☆☆☆
☆☆☆☆☆
☆☆☆☆☆
☆☆☆☆☆

What was your favorite place to visit? Why?

___

Places you ate (restaurants, family's home, etc.):

☆☆☆☆☆
☆☆☆☆☆
☆☆☆☆☆
☆☆☆☆☆
☆☆☆☆☆

What local food specialties did you try?

___

What things do you want to do or see the next time you visit?

___

DID YOU KNOW? The Kentucky Derby, known as "The Most Exciting Two Minutes In Sports," is the oldest continuously held horse race in the country. Since 1875, the Kentucky Derby has been held annually at Churchill Downs in Louisville on the first Saturday in May.

LOUISIANA

State Flag

Admission To Statehood: April 30, 1812 (The 18th State)
Nickname: Pelican State **Capital City:** Baton Rouge
State Motto: Union, Justice, and Confidence
State Bird: Brown Pelican **State Tree:** Bald Cypress
State Flower: Magnolia **State Song:** "Give Me Louisiana"

Date(s) visited:

Who did you travel with?

How did you get there (car, plane, train, etc.):

Place(s) you stayed (hotel, campground, etc.):

☆☆☆☆☆

☆☆☆☆☆

☆☆☆☆☆

Place(s) you visited (landmarks, parks, festivals, points of interest):

☆☆☆☆☆

☆☆☆☆☆

☆☆☆☆☆

☆☆☆☆☆

☆☆☆☆☆

☆☆☆☆☆

What was your favorite place to visit? Why?

___

Places you ate (restaurants, family's home, etc.):

☆☆☆☆☆
☆☆☆☆☆
☆☆☆☆☆
☆☆☆☆☆
☆☆☆☆☆

What local food specialties did you try?

___

What things do you want to do or see the next time you visit?

___

DID YOU KNOW? The first recorded Mardi Gras parade held in New Orleans took place in 1837. The celebration has since become synonymous with the city itself and over one million people travel from all over the world each year to join in the festivities.

MAINE

State Flag

Admission To Statehood: March 15, 1820 (The 23rd State)

Nickname: Pine Tree State   **Capital City:** Augusta

State Motto: Dirigo ("I Direct" or "I Lead")

State Bird: Chickadee   **State Tree:** Eastern White Pine

State Flower: White Pine Cone and Tassel   **State Song:** "State of Maine Song"

Date(s) visited:

Who did you travel with?

How did you get there (car, plane, train, etc.):

Place(s) you stayed (hotel, campground, etc.):

Place(s) you visited (landmarks, parks, festivals, points of interest):

What was your favorite place to visit? Why?

Places you ate (restaurants, family's home, etc.):

☆☆☆☆☆
☆☆☆☆☆
☆☆☆☆☆
☆☆☆☆☆
☆☆☆☆☆

What local food specialties did you try?

What things do you want to do or see the next time you visit?

DID YOU KNOW? The first recorded lobster catch in Maine is from 1605. Maine lobsters were so plentiful they were harvested by hand, and so cheap they were considered to be "poor man's food." Today, around 75 to 80% of American lobsters come from Maine.

MARYLAND

State Flag

Admission To Statehood: April 28, 1788 (The 7th State)
Nickname: Old Line State   **Capital City:** Annapolis
State Motto: Fatti maschii, parole femine (Manly deeds, womanly words)
State Bird: Baltimore Oriole   **State Tree:** White Oak
State Flower: Black-Eyed Susan   **State Song:** "Maryland My Maryland"

Date(s) visited:

Who did you travel with?

How did you get there (car, plane, train, etc.):

Place(s) you stayed (hotel, campground, etc.):

Place(s) you visited (landmarks, parks, festivals, points of interest):

What was your favorite place to visit? Why?

Places you ate (restaurants, family's home, etc.):

☆☆☆☆☆
☆☆☆☆☆
☆☆☆☆☆
☆☆☆☆☆
☆☆☆☆☆

What local food specialties did you try?

What things do you want to do or see the next time you visit?

DID YOU KNOW? Saint Michaels is known as "the town that fooled the British." During the War of 1812, the residents of Saint Michaels, forewarned of a coming attack by the British, hoisted lanterns high in the trees and to the masts of ships, making the town appear "higher." This caused the British to overshoot their cannons, missing the town. Only one house was hit.

MASSACHUSETTS

State Flag

Admission To Statehood: February 6, 1788 (The 6th State)
Nickname: Bay State   **Capital City:** Boston
State Motto: By the sword we seek peace, but peace only under liberty
State Bird: Black-capped Chickadee   **State Tree:** American Elm
State Flower: Mayflower   **State Song:** "All Hail To Massachusetts"

Date(s) visited:

Who did you travel with?

How did you get there (car, plane, train, etc.):

Place(s) you stayed (hotel, campground, etc.):

☆☆☆☆☆

☆☆☆☆☆

☆☆☆☆☆

Place(s) you visited (landmarks, parks, festivals, points of interest):

☆☆☆☆☆

☆☆☆☆☆

☆☆☆☆☆

☆☆☆☆☆

☆☆☆☆☆

☆☆☆☆☆

What was your favorite place to visit? Why?

Places you ate (restaurants, family's home, etc.):

☆☆☆☆☆
☆☆☆☆☆
☆☆☆☆☆
☆☆☆☆☆
☆☆☆☆☆

What local food specialties did you try?

What things do you want to do or see the next time you visit?

DID YOU KNOW? Founded on September 8, 1636, Harvard was the first college established in North America. It's original purpose was to train clergy for the new world. Today, Harvard is considered one of the most prestigious universities in the world.

MICHIGAN

State Flag

Admission To Statehood: January 26, 1837 (The 26th State)
Nickname: Great Lakes State   **Capital City:** Lansing
State Motto: If you seek a pleasant peninsula, look about you
State Bird: American Robin   **State Tree:** Eastern White Pine
State Flower: Apple Blossom   **State Song:** "My Michigan"

Date(s) visited:

Who did you travel with?

How did you get there (car, plane, train, etc.):

Place(s) you stayed (hotel, campground, etc.):

Place(s) you visited (landmarks, parks, festivals, points of interest):

What was your favorite place to visit? Why?

_____
_____
_____

Places you ate (restaurants, family's home, etc.):

_____ ☆☆☆☆☆
_____ ☆☆☆☆☆
_____ ☆☆☆☆☆
_____ ☆☆☆☆☆
_____ ☆☆☆☆☆

What local food specialties did you try?

_____
_____

What things do you want to do or see the next time you visit?

_____
_____
_____
_____

DID YOU KNOW? Explore the numerous waterfalls scattered across Michigan's Upper Peninsula. The best time to visit the falls is in the spring when area snowmelt causes rivers and streams to swell and the waterfalls roar to life.

MINNESOTA

State Flag

Admission To Statehood: May 11, 1858 (The 32nd State)

Nickname: North Star State   **Capital City:** Saint Paul

State Motto: L'Étoile du Nord (The star of the North)

State Bird: Common Loon   **State Tree:** Red Pine

State Flower: Pink and White Lady's Slipper   **State Song:** "Hail Minnesota"

Date(s) visited: _____

Who did you travel with? _____

How did you get there (car, plane, train, etc.): _____

Place(s) you stayed (hotel, campground, etc.):

☆☆☆☆☆

☆☆☆☆☆

☆☆☆☆☆

Place(s) you visited (landmarks, parks, festivals, points of interest):

☆☆☆☆☆

☆☆☆☆☆

☆☆☆☆☆

☆☆☆☆☆

☆☆☆☆☆

☆☆☆☆☆

What was your favorite place to visit? Why?

Places you ate (restaurants, family's home, etc.):

☆☆☆☆☆

☆☆☆☆☆

☆☆☆☆☆

☆☆☆☆☆

☆☆☆☆☆

What local food specialties did you try?

What things do you want to do or see the next time you visit?

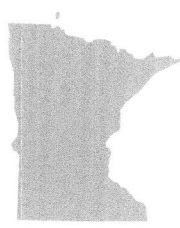

DID YOU KNOW? The Mall of America in Bloomington is a whopping 4,870,000 sq. ft. (that's 96.4 acres)! It boasts a 7 acre indoor theme park, an aquarium, miniature golf, a comedy club, and countless shopping and dining opportunities.

MISSISSIPPI

State Flag

Admission To Statehood: December 10, 1817 (The 20th State)
Nickname: Magnolia State   **Capital City:** Jackson
State Motto: Virtute et armis (By valor and arms)
State Bird: Northern Mockingbird   **State Tree:** Southern Magnolia
State Flower: Magnolia   **State Song:** "Go, Mississippi"

Date(s) visited:

Who did you travel with?

How did you get there (car, plane, train, etc.):

Place(s) you stayed (hotel, campground, etc.):

☆☆☆☆☆

☆☆☆☆☆

☆☆☆☆☆

Place(s) you visited (landmarks, parks, festivals, points of interest):

☆☆☆☆☆

☆☆☆☆☆

☆☆☆☆☆

☆☆☆☆☆

☆☆☆☆☆

☆☆☆☆☆

What was your favorite place to visit? Why? _____
_____
_____
_____

Places you ate (restaurants, family's home, etc.):

_____ ☆☆☆☆☆
_____ ☆☆☆☆☆
_____ ☆☆☆☆☆
_____ ☆☆☆☆☆
_____ ☆☆☆☆☆

What local food specialties did you try? _____
_____
_____

What things do you want to do or see the next time you visit? _____
_____
_____
_____
_____

DID YOU KNOW? The Mississippi Sandhill Crane, the rarest of all North American cranes, lives only in the unique wet pine savannas of Jackson County, Mississippi. These endangered cranes stand about 3 to 4 feet tall and have a wingspan of over 7 feet.

MISSOURI

State Flag

Admission To Statehood: August 10, 1821 (The 24th State)
Nickname: Show Me State **Capital City:** Jefferson City
State Motto: Let the welfare of the people be the supreme law
State Bird: Eastern Bluebird **State Tree:** Flowering Dogwood
State Flower: Hawthorn **State Song:** "Missouri Waltz"

Date(s) visited:

Who did you travel with?

How did you get there (car, plane, train, etc.):

Place(s) you stayed (hotel, campground, etc.):

☆☆☆☆☆
☆☆☆☆☆
☆☆☆☆☆

Place(s) you visited (landmarks, parks, festivals, points of interest):

☆☆☆☆☆
☆☆☆☆☆
☆☆☆☆☆
☆☆☆☆☆
☆☆☆☆☆
☆☆☆☆☆

What was your favorite place to visit? Why?

Places you ate (restaurants, family's home, etc.):

☆☆☆☆☆
☆☆☆☆☆
☆☆☆☆☆
☆☆☆☆☆
☆☆☆☆☆

What local food specialties did you try?

What things do you want to do or see the next time you visit?

DID YOU KNOW? Gateway Arch, which stands alongside the Mississippi River in St. Louis, was designed to pay tribute to the role the city played as the "Gateway to the West" during the westward expansion of the country.

MONTANA

State Flag

Admission To Statehood: November 8, 1889 (The 41st State)

Nickname: Treasure State **Capital City:** Helena

State Motto: Oro y Plata (Gold and Silver)

State Bird: Western Meadowlark **State Tree:** Ponderosa Pine

State Flower: Bitterroot **State Song:** "Montana"

Date(s) visited:

Who did you travel with?

How did you get there (car, plane, train, etc.):

Place(s) you stayed (hotel, campground, etc.):

☆☆☆☆☆

☆☆☆☆☆

☆☆☆☆☆

Place(s) you visited (landmarks, parks, festivals, points of interest):

☆☆☆☆☆

☆☆☆☆☆

☆☆☆☆☆

☆☆☆☆☆

☆☆☆☆☆

☆☆☆☆☆

What was your favorite place to visit? Why?

Places you ate (restaurants, family's home, etc.):

☆☆☆☆☆
☆☆☆☆☆
☆☆☆☆☆
☆☆☆☆☆
☆☆☆☆☆

What local food specialties did you try?

What things do you want to do or see the next time you visit?

DID YOU KNOW? Virginia City was founded in 1863 after a couple of miners discovered gold nearby. It quickly became a boomtown and served as the capital of Montana Territory from 1865 to 1875. Now Virginia City and the surrounding area is a National Historic Landmark District.

NEBRASKA

State Flag

Admission To Statehood: March 1, 1867 (The 37th State)

Nickname: Cornhusker State   **Capital City:** Lincoln

State Motto: Equality Before The Law

State Bird: Western Meadowlark   **State Tree:** Eastern Cottonwood

State Flower: Goldenrod   **State Song:** "Beautiful Nebraska"

Date(s) visited:

Who did you travel with?

How did you get there (car, plane, train, etc.):

Place(s) you stayed (hotel, campground, etc.):

☆☆☆☆☆

☆☆☆☆☆

☆☆☆☆☆

Place(s) you visited (landmarks, parks, festivals, points of interest):

☆☆☆☆☆

☆☆☆☆☆

☆☆☆☆☆

☆☆☆☆☆

☆☆☆☆☆

☆☆☆☆☆

What was your favorite place to visit? Why?

Places you ate (restaurants, family's home, etc.):

☆☆☆☆☆
☆☆☆☆☆
☆☆☆☆☆
☆☆☆☆☆
☆☆☆☆☆

What local food specialties did you try?

What things do you want to do or see the next time you visit?

DID YOU KNOW? Chimney Rock, a geological formation rising almost 300 feet above the surrounding valley in western Nebraska, served as a landmark to mid-19th century explorers. It was the most frequently mentioned landmark in journals of Oregon Trail travelers.

NEVADA

State Flag

Admission To Statehood: October 31, 1864 (The 36th State)

Nickname: Silver State   **Capital City:** Carson City

State Motto: All For Our Country   **State Tree:** Bristlecone Pine and Single-leaf Pinyon

State Bird: Mountain Bluebird

State Flower: Big Sagebrush   **State Song:** "Home Means Nevada"

Date(s) visited: _____

Who did you travel with? _____

How did you get there (car, plane, train, etc.): _____

Place(s) you stayed (hotel, campground, etc.):

☆☆☆☆☆
☆☆☆☆☆
☆☆☆☆☆

Place(s) you visited (landmarks, parks, festivals, points of interest):

☆☆☆☆☆
☆☆☆☆☆
☆☆☆☆☆
☆☆☆☆☆
☆☆☆☆☆
☆☆☆☆☆

What was your favorite place to visit? Why?

Places you ate (restaurants, family's home, etc.):

☆☆☆☆☆
☆☆☆☆☆
☆☆☆☆☆
☆☆☆☆☆
☆☆☆☆☆

What local food specialties did you try?

What things do you want to do or see the next time you visit?

DID YOU KNOW? In 1864, the longest Morse code telegram in history was sent from Carson City, NV. It was the Nevada State Constitution. The document took 7 hours to send and had to be relayed through 3 other cities before reaching Washington, DC where it was made into a 175 page transcription (16,543 words) and presented to President Abraham Lincoln.

NEW HAMPSHIRE

State Flag

Admission To Statehood: June 21, 1788 (The 9th State)
Nickname: Granite State   **Capital City:** Concord
State Motto: Live Free Or Die
State Bird: Purple Finch   **State Tree:** Paper Birch
State Flower: Purple Lilac   **State Song:** "Old New Hampshire"

Date(s) visited:

Who did you travel with?

How did you get there (car, plane, train, etc.):

Place(s) you stayed (hotel, campground, etc.):

☆☆☆☆☆
☆☆☆☆☆
☆☆☆☆☆

Place(s) you visited (landmarks, parks, festivals, points of interest):

☆☆☆☆☆
☆☆☆☆☆
☆☆☆☆☆
☆☆☆☆☆
☆☆☆☆☆
☆☆☆☆☆

What was your favorite place to visit? Why?

Places you ate (restaurants, family's home, etc.):

☆☆☆☆☆

☆☆☆☆☆

☆☆☆☆☆

☆☆☆☆☆

☆☆☆☆☆

What local food specialties did you try?

What things do you want to do or see the next time you visit?

DID YOU KNOW? Mount Washington, elevation 6288 feet, is the highest peak in the northeast. But you don't have to hike or even drive to the summit. You can take the cog railway instead. The Washington Cog Railway, the first of if its kind, has been transporting visitors up Mount Washington since 1869.

NEW JERSEY

State Flag

Admission To Statehood: December 18, 1787 (The 3rd State)
Nickname: Garden State **Capital City:** Trenton
State Motto: Liberty and Prosperity
State Bird: Eastern Goldfinch **State Tree:** Northern Red Oak
State Flower: Violet **State Song:** (unofficial) "I'm From New Jersey"

Date(s) visited:

Who did you travel with?

How did you get there (car, plane, train, etc.):

Place(s) you stayed (hotel, campground, etc.):

☆☆☆☆☆

☆☆☆☆☆

☆☆☆☆☆

Place(s) you visited (landmarks, parks, festivals, points of interest):

☆☆☆☆☆

☆☆☆☆☆

☆☆☆☆☆

☆☆☆☆☆

☆☆☆☆☆

☆☆☆☆☆

What was your favorite place to visit? Why?

Places you ate (restaurants, family's home, etc.):

☆☆☆☆☆
☆☆☆☆☆
☆☆☆☆☆
☆☆☆☆☆
☆☆☆☆☆

What local food specialties did you try?

What things do you want to do or see the next time you visit?

DID YOU KNOW? In 1858, the discovery of a nearly complete dinosaur skeleton occurred in Haddonfield, New Jersey. The skeleton was that of a Hadrosaurus, now the "official" state dinosaur of New Jersey.

NEW MEXICO

State Flag

Admission To Statehood: January 6, 1912 (The 47th State)
Nickname: The Land of Enchantment   **Capital City:** Santa Fe
State Motto: Crecit eundo (It grows as it goes)
State Bird: Roadrunner   **State Tree:** Piñon Pine
State Flower: Yucca Flower   **State Song:** "O, Fair New Mexico"

Date(s) visited:

Who did you travel with?

How did you get there (car, plane, train, etc.):

Place(s) you stayed (hotel, campground, etc.):

Place(s) you visited (landmarks, parks, festivals, points of interest):

What was your favorite place to visit? Why?

Places you ate (restaurants, family's home, etc.):

☆☆☆☆☆
☆☆☆☆☆
☆☆☆☆☆
☆☆☆☆☆
☆☆☆☆☆

What local food specialties did you try?

What things do you want to do or see the next time you visit?

DID YOU KNOW? Hatch, NM is know as the "Green Chile Capital of the World." New Mexico grows green chiles in many different areas within its borders, but Hatch green chiles are grown only in the Hatch Valley along the Rio Grande River.

NEW YORK

State Flag

Admission To Statehood: July 26, 1788 (The 11th State)
Nickname: Empire State **Capital City:** Albany
State Motto: Excelsior! (Ever Upward!)
State Bird: Eastern Bluebird **State Tree:** Sugar Maple
State Flower: Rose **State Song:** "I Love New York"

Date(s) visited: _____

Who did you travel with? _____

How did you get there (car, plane, train, etc.): _____

Place(s) you stayed (hotel, campground, etc.):

☆☆☆☆☆

☆☆☆☆☆

☆☆☆☆☆

Place(s) you visited (landmarks, parks, festivals, points of interest):

☆☆☆☆☆

☆☆☆☆☆

☆☆☆☆☆

☆☆☆☆☆

☆☆☆☆☆

☆☆☆☆☆

What was your favorite place to visit? Why? _____

_____

_____

_____

Places you ate (restaurants, family's home, etc.):

_____ ☆☆☆☆☆

_____ ☆☆☆☆☆

_____ ☆☆☆☆☆

_____ ☆☆☆☆☆

_____ ☆☆☆☆☆

What local food specialties did you try? _____

_____

_____

What things do you want to do or see the next time you visit? _____

_____

_____

_____

_____

DID YOU KNOW? New York State is home to almost 60 native species of orchids. Some are quite common, but many are considered to be endangered or threatened.

NORTH CAROLINA

State Flag

Admission To Statehood: November 21, 1789 (The 12th State)
Nickname: Tar Heel State   **Capital City:** Raleigh
State Motto: Esse quam videri (To be, rather than to seem)
State Bird: Cardinal   **State Tree:** Pine
State Flower: Dogwood   **State Song:** "The Old North State"

Date(s) visited:

Who did you travel with?

How did you get there (car, plane, train, etc.):

Place(s) you stayed (hotel, campground, etc.):

☆☆☆☆☆

☆☆☆☆☆

☆☆☆☆☆

Place(s) you visited (landmarks, parks, festivals, points of interest):

☆☆☆☆☆

☆☆☆☆☆

☆☆☆☆☆

☆☆☆☆☆

☆☆☆☆☆

☆☆☆☆☆

What was your favorite place to visit? Why?

Places you ate (restaurants, family's home, etc.):

☆☆☆☆☆
☆☆☆☆☆
☆☆☆☆☆
☆☆☆☆☆
☆☆☆☆☆

What local food specialties did you try?

What things do you want to do or see the next time you visit?

DID YOU KNOW? There is some uncertainty about where the "Tar Heels" nickname originated, but by the late 1800s it had evolved into an expression of state pride. Being a "Tar Heel" was a badge of honor.

NORTH DAKOTA

State Flag

Admission To Statehood: November 2, 1889 (The 39th or 40th State)
Nickname: Peace Garden State   **Capital City:** Bismark
State Motto: Liberty and union, now and forever, one and inseparable
State Bird: Western Meadowlark   **State Tree:** American Elm
State Flower: Wild Prairie Rose   **State Song:** "North Dakota Hymn"

Date(s) visited:

Who did you travel with?

How did you get there (car, plane, train, etc.):

Place(s) you stayed (hotel, campground, etc.):

☆☆☆☆☆

☆☆☆☆☆

☆☆☆☆☆

Place(s) you visited (landmarks, parks, festivals, points of interest):

☆☆☆☆☆

☆☆☆☆☆

☆☆☆☆☆

☆☆☆☆☆

☆☆☆☆☆

☆☆☆☆☆

What was your favorite place to visit? Why?

Places you ate (restaurants, family's home, etc.):

☆☆☆☆☆
☆☆☆☆☆
☆☆☆☆☆
☆☆☆☆☆
☆☆☆☆☆

What local food specialties did you try?

What things do you want to do or see the next time you visit?

DID YOU KNOW? Interested in paleontology? Join a fossil dig in North Dakota! Because the area has an environment favorable for preserving its prehistoric residents, North Dakota is known for having an abundance of fossilized plants and animals.

OHIO

State Flag

Admission To Statehood: March 1, 1803 (The 17th State)
Nickname: Buckeye State   **Capital City:** Columbus
State Motto: With God, All Things Are Possible
State Bird: Cardinal   **State Tree:** Ohio Buckeye
State Flower: Scarlet Carnation **State Song:** "Beautiful Ohio"

Date(s) visited:

Who did you travel with?

How did you get there (car, plane, train, etc.):

Place(s) you stayed (hotel, campground, etc.):

☆☆☆☆☆

☆☆☆☆☆

☆☆☆☆☆

Place(s) you visited (landmarks, parks, festivals, points of interest):

☆☆☆☆☆

☆☆☆☆☆

☆☆☆☆☆

☆☆☆☆☆

☆☆☆☆☆

☆☆☆☆☆

What was your favorite place to visit? Why?

Places you ate (restaurants, family's home, etc.):

☆☆☆☆☆

☆☆☆☆☆

☆☆☆☆☆

☆☆☆☆☆

☆☆☆☆☆

What local food specialties did you try?

What things do you want to do or see the next time you visit?

DID YOU KNOW? In 2011, fact checkers determined that 184,900,000 people, 59.9% of the country's population at that time, lived within a 600-mile radius of Ohio. The area included the eastern coast from southern Maine to northern Florida and portions west of the Mississippi River.

OKLAHOMA

State Flag

Admission To Statehood: November 16, 1907 (The 46th State)
Nickname: Sooner State   **Capital City:** Oklahoma City
State Motto: Labor omnia vincit (Labor Conquers All Things)
State Bird: Scissor-tailed Flycatcher   **State Tree:** Eastern Redbud
State Flower: Oklahoma Rose   **State Song:** "Oklahoma"

Date(s) visited:

Who did you travel with?

How did you get there (car, plane, train, etc.):

Place(s) you stayed (hotel, campground, etc.):

Place(s) you visited (landmarks, parks, festivals, points of interest):

What was your favorite place to visit? Why?

Places you ate (restaurants, family's home, etc.):

☆☆☆☆☆
☆☆☆☆☆
☆☆☆☆☆
☆☆☆☆☆
☆☆☆☆☆

What local food specialties did you try?

What things do you want to do or see the next time you visit?

DID YOU KNOW? In 1889, Oklahoma was opened to settlers in the first, and most famous, "Land Rush". An estimated 50,000 people participated in this frenzied race for a chance at land ownership. By the end of the day, 2 million acres had been claimed.

OREGON

State Flag

Admission To Statehood: February 14, 1859 (The 33rd State)
Nickname: Beaver State **Capital City:** Salem
State Motto: Alis volat propriis (She flies with her own wings)
State Bird: Western Meadowlark **State Tree:** Douglas Fir
State Flower: Oregon Grape **State Song:** "Oregon, My Oregon"

Date(s) visited:

Who did you travel with?

How did you get there (car, plane, train, etc.):

Place(s) you stayed (hotel, campground, etc.):

Place(s) you visited (landmarks, parks, festivals, points of interest):

What was your favorite place to visit? Why?

Places you ate (restaurants, family's home, etc.):

☆☆☆☆☆
☆☆☆☆☆
☆☆☆☆☆
☆☆☆☆☆
☆☆☆☆☆

What local food specialties did you try?

What things do you want to do or see the next time you visit?

DID YOU KNOW? There are nine historic lighthouses dotting the rugged Oregon coastline. These iconic structures, built between 1870 and 1934, are all on the National Register of Historic Places.

PENNSYLVANIA

State Flag

Admission To Statehood: December 12, 1787 (The 2nd State)
Nickname: Keystone State **Capital City:** Harrisburg
State Motto: Virtue, Liberty, and Independence
State Bird: Ruffled Grouse **State Tree:** Eastern Hemlock
State Flower: Mountain Laurel **State Song:** "Pennsylvania"

Date(s) visited: _____

Who did you travel with? _____

How did you get there (car, plane, train, etc.): _____

Place(s) you stayed (hotel, campground, etc.):

☆☆☆☆☆
☆☆☆☆☆
☆☆☆☆☆

Place(s) you visited (landmarks, parks, festivals, points of interest):

☆☆☆☆☆
☆☆☆☆☆
☆☆☆☆☆
☆☆☆☆☆
☆☆☆☆☆
☆☆☆☆☆

What was your favorite place to visit? Why?

_____

_____

_____

Places you ate (restaurants, family's home, etc.):

_____	☆☆☆☆☆
_____	☆☆☆☆☆
_____	☆☆☆☆☆
_____	☆☆☆☆☆
_____	☆☆☆☆☆

What local food specialties did you try? _____

_____

_____

What things do you want to do or see the next time you visit? _____

_____

_____

_____

_____

DID YOU KNOW? When British troops threatened to capture Philadelphia in 1777, the Liberty Bell was sent into into hiding in Allentown and kept there during the British occupation of Pennsylvania. The bell was returned nine months later in 1778.

RHODE ISLAND

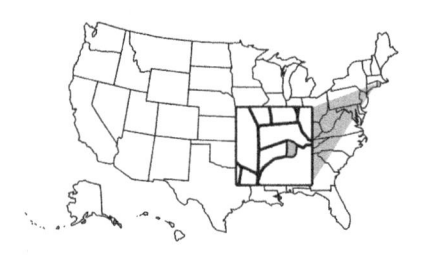

State Flag

Admission To Statehood: May 29, 1790 (The 13th State)
Nickname: Ocean State   **Capital City:** Providence
State Motto: Hope
State Bird: Rhode Island Red   **State Tree:** Red Maple
State Flower: Violet   **State Song:** "Rhode Island's It For Me"

Date(s) visited: _____

Who did you travel with? _____

How did you get there (car, plane, train, etc.): _____

Place(s) you stayed (hotel, campground, etc.):

☆☆☆☆☆
☆☆☆☆☆
☆☆☆☆☆

Place(s) you visited (landmarks, parks, festivals, points of interest):

☆☆☆☆☆
☆☆☆☆☆
☆☆☆☆☆
☆☆☆☆☆
☆☆☆☆☆
☆☆☆☆☆

What was your favorite place to visit? Why?

Places you ate (restaurants, family's home, etc.):

☆☆☆☆☆
☆☆☆☆☆
☆☆☆☆☆
☆☆☆☆☆
☆☆☆☆☆

What local food specialties did you try?

What things do you want to do or see the next time you visit?

DID YOU KNOW? The Masonic Temple in Warren, chartered in the 1790s, is believed to have been built using timbers from British ships that were sunk in the Newport Harbor during the Revolutionary War. To transport the timbers, they were floated up Narragansett Bay and into the Warren River.

SOUTH CAROLINA

State Flag

Admission To Statehood: May 23, 1788 (The 8th State)
Nickname: Palmetto State   **Capital City:** Columbia
State Motto: While I breathe, I hope
State Bird: Carolina Wren   **State Tree:** Sabal Palm
State Flower: Yellow Jessamine   **State Song:** "Carolina"

Date(s) visited:

Who did you travel with?

How did you get there (car, plane, train, etc.):

Place(s) you stayed (hotel, campground, etc.):

Place(s) you visited (landmarks, parks, festivals, points of interest):

What was your favorite place to visit? Why? _____

_____
_____
_____

Places you ate (restaurants, family's home, etc.):

Place	Rating
_____	☆☆☆☆☆
_____	☆☆☆☆☆
_____	☆☆☆☆☆
_____	☆☆☆☆☆
_____	☆☆☆☆☆

What local food specialties did you try? _____

_____
_____

What things do you want to do or see the next time you visit? _____

_____
_____
_____
_____

DID YOU KNOW? Although Georgia is nicknamed the "Peach State", South Carolina produces far more of the tasty fruit each year. In fact, South Carolina ranks #2 in peach production in the nation (behind California).

SOUTH DAKOTA

State Flag

Admission To Statehood: November 2, 1889 (The 39th or 40th State)
Nickname: Mount Rushmore State   **Capital City:** Pierre
State Motto: Under God the people rule
State Bird: Ring-necked Pheasant   **State Tree:** Black Hills Spruce
State Flower: Pasque Flower   **State Song:** "Hail, South Dakota"

Date(s) visited:

Who did you travel with?

How did you get there (car, plane, train, etc.):

Place(s) you stayed (hotel, campground, etc.):

☆☆☆☆☆
☆☆☆☆☆
☆☆☆☆☆

Place(s) you visited (landmarks, parks, festivals, points of interest):

☆☆☆☆☆
☆☆☆☆☆
☆☆☆☆☆
☆☆☆☆☆
☆☆☆☆☆
☆☆☆☆☆

What was your favorite place to visit? Why?

Places you ate (restaurants, family's home, etc.):

☆☆☆☆☆
☆☆☆☆☆
☆☆☆☆☆
☆☆☆☆☆
☆☆☆☆☆

What local food specialties did you try?

What things do you want to do or see the next time you visit?

DID YOU KNOW? Work on Mount Rushmore began in 1927. It took 14 years at a cost of nearly $1 million dollars. Every year, approximately three million visitors travel from all over the world to the Black Hills of South Dakota to view what has been called "the world's greatest mountain carving."

TENNESSEE

State Flag

Admission To Statehood: June 1, 1796 (The 16th State)
Nickname: Volunteer State   **Capital City:** Nashville
State Motto: Agriculture and Commerce
State Bird: Mockingbird   **State Tree:** Tulip Tree
State Flower: Iris   **State Song:** "My Homeland, Tennessee" (the first of 10 official state songs)

Date(s) visited:

Who did you travel with?

How did you get there (car, plane, train, etc.):

Place(s) you stayed (hotel, campground, etc.):

☆☆☆☆☆

☆☆☆☆☆

☆☆☆☆☆

Place(s) you visited (landmarks, parks, festivals, points of interest):

☆☆☆☆☆

☆☆☆☆☆

☆☆☆☆☆

☆☆☆☆☆

☆☆☆☆☆

☆☆☆☆☆

What was your favorite place to visit? Why?

_____
_____
_____

Places you ate (restaurants, family's home, etc.):

_____ ☆☆☆☆☆
_____ ☆☆☆☆☆
_____ ☆☆☆☆☆
_____ ☆☆☆☆☆
_____ ☆☆☆☆☆

What local food specialties did you try?

_____
_____

What things do you want to do or see the next time you visit?

_____
_____
_____
_____

DID YOU KNOW? As of 2019, Tennessee had 10 official state songs beginning with "My Homeland, Tennessee" that was adopted as the official song in 1925. Other state songs include "When It's Iris Time in Tennessee" (1935), "My Tennessee" (1955), "Tennessee Waltz" (1965), "Rocky Top" (1982), "Tennessee" (1992), "The Pride of Tennessee" (1996), "A Tennessee Bicentennial Rap: 1796-1996" (1996), "Smoky Mountain Rain" (2010), and "Tennessee" (2012).

TEXAS

State Flag

Admission To Statehood: December 29, 1845 (The 28th State)

Nickname: Lone Star State **Capital City:** Austin

State Motto: Friendship

State Bird: Northern Mockingbird **State Tree:** Pecan

State Flower: Bluebonnet **State Song:** "Texas, Our Texas"

Date(s) visited:

Who did you travel with?

How did you get there (car, plane, train, etc.):

Place(s) you stayed (hotel, campground, etc.):

☆☆☆☆☆
☆☆☆☆☆
☆☆☆☆☆

Place(s) you visited (landmarks, parks, festivals, points of interest):

☆☆☆☆☆
☆☆☆☆☆
☆☆☆☆☆
☆☆☆☆☆
☆☆☆☆☆
☆☆☆☆☆

What was your favorite place to visit? Why?

Places you ate (restaurants, family's home, etc.):

☆☆☆☆☆
☆☆☆☆☆
☆☆☆☆☆
☆☆☆☆☆
☆☆☆☆☆

What local food specialties did you try?

What things do you want to do or see the next time you visit?

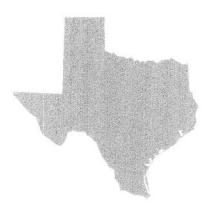

DID YOU KNOW? The state of Texas is the largest state in the contiguous United States, second only to Alaska. In fact, it accounts for 7% of the country's total land area. It is so large that El Paso, on the western side of Texas, is closer (as the crow flies) to Needles, California than it is to Dallas.

UTAH

State Flag

Admission To Statehood: January 4, 1896 (The 45th State)
Nickname: Beehive State   **Capital City:** Salt Lake City
State Motto: Industry
State Bird: California Gull   **State Tree:** Quaking Aspen
State Flower: Sego Lily   **State Song:** "Utah...This Is The Place"

Date(s) visited:

Who did you travel with?

How did you get there (car, plane, train, etc.):

Place(s) you stayed (hotel, campground, etc.):

☆☆☆☆☆

☆☆☆☆☆

☆☆☆☆☆

Place(s) you visited (landmarks, parks, festivals, points of interest):

☆☆☆☆☆

☆☆☆☆☆

☆☆☆☆☆

☆☆☆☆☆

☆☆☆☆☆

☆☆☆☆☆

What was your favorite place to visit? Why?

Places you ate (restaurants, family's home, etc.):

☆☆☆☆☆
☆☆☆☆☆
☆☆☆☆☆
☆☆☆☆☆
☆☆☆☆☆

What local food specialties did you try?

What things do you want to do or see the next time you visit?

DID YOU KNOW? Utah has five National Parks, six National Forests, seven National Monuments and two National Recreation Areas. There are also 43 state parks. Be sure to set aside time for all the adventuring while traveling through Utah!

VERMONT

State Flag

Admission To Statehood: March 4, 1791 (The 14th State)
Nickname: Green Mountain State   **Capital City:** Montpelier
State Motto: Freedom and Unity
State Bird: Hermit Thrush   **State Tree:** Sugar Maple
State Flower: Red Clover   **State Song:** "These Green Mountains"

Date(s) visited:

Who did you travel with?

How did you get there (car, plane, train, etc.):

Place(s) you stayed (hotel, campground, etc.):

☆☆☆☆☆

☆☆☆☆☆

☆☆☆☆☆

Place(s) you visited (landmarks, parks, festivals, points of interest):

☆☆☆☆☆

☆☆☆☆☆

☆☆☆☆☆

☆☆☆☆☆

☆☆☆☆☆

☆☆☆☆☆

What was your favorite place to visit? Why? _____

_____

_____

_____

Places you ate (restaurants, family's home, etc.):

_____	☆☆☆☆☆
_____	☆☆☆☆☆
_____	☆☆☆☆☆
_____	☆☆☆☆☆
_____	☆☆☆☆☆

What local food specialties did you try? _____

_____

_____

What things do you want to do or see the next time you visit? _____

_____

_____

_____

_____

DID YOU KNOW? On average, one maple tree will supply 10 to 20 gallons of sap in a season. It takes roughly 40 gallons of sap to make just one gallon of syrup. Vermont produces over half a million gallons of maple syrup annually, which equals 20 MILLION gallons of sap harvested every year!

VIRGINIA

State Flag

Admission To Statehood: June 25, 1788 (The 10th State)
Nickname: Old Dominion State   **Capital City:** Richmond
State Motto: Sic semper tyrannis (Thus always to tyrants)
State Bird: Northern Cardinal   **State Tree:** Flowering Dogwood
State Flower: Dogwood   **State Song:** "Sweet Virginia Breeze"

Date(s) visited:

Who did you travel with?

How did you get there (car, plane, train, etc.):

Place(s) you stayed (hotel, campground, etc.):

☆☆☆☆☆

☆☆☆☆☆

☆☆☆☆☆

Place(s) you visited (landmarks, parks, festivals, points of interest):

☆☆☆☆☆

☆☆☆☆☆

☆☆☆☆☆

☆☆☆☆☆

☆☆☆☆☆

☆☆☆☆☆

What was your favorite place to visit? Why?

Places you ate (restaurants, family's home, etc.):

☆☆☆☆☆
☆☆☆☆☆
☆☆☆☆☆
☆☆☆☆☆
☆☆☆☆☆

What local food specialties did you try?

What things do you want to do or see the next time you visit?

DID YOU KNOW? Virginia is known as the "Birthplace of a nation." Jamestown, Virginia, established in 1607, was the first successful permanent English settlement in North America. Jamestown also served as the capital the Virginia colony until 1699 when the capital moved to Williamsburg and Jamestown was abandoned.

WASHINGTON

State Flag

Admission To Statehood: November 11, 1889 (The 42nd State)
Nickname: Evergreen State   **Capital City:** Olympia
State Motto: Al-ki (By and by)
State Bird: Willow Goldfinch   **State Tree:** Western Hemlock
State Flower: Coast Rhododendron   **State Song:** "Washington, My Home"

Date(s) visited:

Who did you travel with?

How did you get there (car, plane, train, etc.):

Place(s) you stayed (hotel, campground, etc.):

☆☆☆☆☆

☆☆☆☆☆

☆☆☆☆☆

Place(s) you visited (landmarks, parks, festivals, points of interest):

☆☆☆☆☆

☆☆☆☆☆

☆☆☆☆☆

☆☆☆☆☆

☆☆☆☆☆

☆☆☆☆☆

What was your favorite place to visit? Why? _____

_____

_____

_____

Places you ate (restaurants, family's home, etc.):

_____ ☆☆☆☆☆

_____ ☆☆☆☆☆

_____ ☆☆☆☆☆

_____ ☆☆☆☆☆

_____ ☆☆☆☆☆

What local food specialties did you try? _____

_____

_____

What things do you want to do or see the next time you visit? _____

_____

_____

_____

_____

DID YOU KNOW? Before Washington became a state, a proposed name for Washington Territory was "Columbia Territory" but it was thought the name might be confused with the District of Columbia. It was instead named in honor of George Washington. It is the only U.S. state to be named after a president.

WEST VIRGINIA

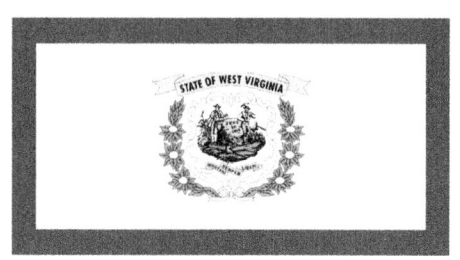

State Flag

Admission To Statehood: June 20, 1863 (The 35th State)
Nickname: Mountain State **Capital City:** Charleston
State Motto: Montani semper liberi (Mountaineers are always free)
State Bird: Northern Cardinal **State Tree:** Sugar Maple
State Flower: Rhododendron **State Song:** "West Virginia Hills"

Date(s) visited:

Who did you travel with?

How did you get there (car, plane, train, etc.):

Place(s) you stayed (hotel, campground, etc.):

☆☆☆☆☆

☆☆☆☆☆

☆☆☆☆☆

Place(s) you visited (landmarks, parks, festivals, points of interest):

☆☆☆☆☆

☆☆☆☆☆

☆☆☆☆☆

☆☆☆☆☆

☆☆☆☆☆

☆☆☆☆☆

What was your favorite place to visit? Why?

Places you ate (restaurants, family's home, etc.):

☆☆☆☆☆
☆☆☆☆☆
☆☆☆☆☆
☆☆☆☆☆
☆☆☆☆☆

What local food specialties did you try?

What things do you want to do or see the next time you visit?

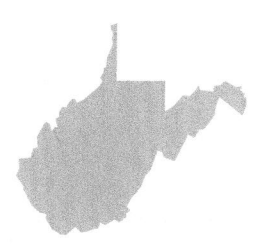

DID YOU KNOW? West Virginia is the third most heavily forested state in the country (behind Maine and New Hampshire). Nearly 78% of West Virginia's 24,000 square miles is covered by forests. That's over 11 million acres of trees!

WISCONSIN

State Flag

Admission To Statehood: May 29, 1848 (The 30th State)
Nickname: Badger State   **Capital City:** Madison
State Motto: Forward
State Bird: American Robin   **State Tree:** Sugar Maple
State Flower: Wood Violet   **State Song:** "On, Wisconsin!"

Date(s) visited:

Who did you travel with?

How did you get there (car, plane, train, etc.):

Place(s) you stayed (hotel, campground, etc.):

Place(s) you visited (landmarks, parks, festivals, points of interest):

What was your favorite place to visit? Why?

Places you ate (restaurants, family's home, etc.):

☆☆☆☆☆
☆☆☆☆☆
☆☆☆☆☆
☆☆☆☆☆
☆☆☆☆☆

What local food specialties did you try?

What things do you want to do or see the next time you visit?

DID YOU KNOW: The sale and use of yellow margarine was banned from 1895 to 1967. Wisconsinites would smuggle it in from bordering states. Even today, some margarine restrictions remain. It is illegal for a restaurant to serve margarine as a butter substitute unless a diner requests it.

WYOMING

State Flag

Admission To Statehood: July 10, 1890 (The 44th State)
Nickname: Equality State   **Capital City:** Cheyenne
State Motto: Equal Rights
State Bird: Western Meadowlark   **State Tree:** Plains Cottonwood
State Flower: Indian Paintbrush   **State Song:** "Wyoming"

Date(s) visited:

Who did you travel with?

How did you get there (car, plane, train, etc.):

Place(s) you stayed (hotel, campground, etc.):

☆☆☆☆☆

☆☆☆☆☆

☆☆☆☆☆

Place(s) you visited (landmarks, parks, festivals, points of interest):

☆☆☆☆☆

☆☆☆☆☆

☆☆☆☆☆

☆☆☆☆☆

☆☆☆☆☆

☆☆☆☆☆

What was your favorite place to visit? Why?

Places you ate (restaurants, family's home, etc.):

☆☆☆☆☆
☆☆☆☆☆
☆☆☆☆☆
☆☆☆☆☆
☆☆☆☆☆

What local food specialties did you try?

What things do you want to do or see the next time you visit?

DID YOU KNOW? On December 10, 1869, the Territory of Wyoming became the first to grant unrestrictive voting rights to women. Wyoming insisted on retaining that right as a condition of statehood and in 1890, upon joining the Union, became the first state allowing women the right to vote, 30 years before the 19th Amendment was ratified.

WASHINGTON, D.C.

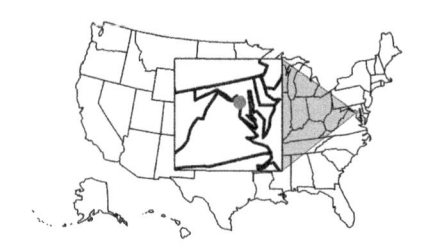

District Flag

Established: 1801 as "District of Columbia", 1871 as "Washington, D.C."
Nickname: "The Federal City" or "The District"
Official Bird: Wood Thrush
Official Flower: American Beauty Rose
Official Tree: Scarlet Oak

Date(s) visited:

Who did you travel with?

How did you get there (car, plane, train, etc.):

Place(s) you stayed (hotel, campground, etc.):

☆☆☆☆☆
☆☆☆☆☆
☆☆☆☆☆

Place(s) you visited (landmarks, parks, festivals, points of interest):

☆☆☆☆☆
☆☆☆☆☆
☆☆☆☆☆
☆☆☆☆☆
☆☆☆☆☆
☆☆☆☆☆

What was your favorite place to visit? Why?

Places you ate (restaurants, family's home, etc.):

☆☆☆☆☆
☆☆☆☆☆
☆☆☆☆☆
☆☆☆☆☆
☆☆☆☆☆

What local food specialties did you try?

What things do you want to do or see the next time you visit?

DID YOU KNOW? Have you ever noticed the Washington Monument is two different colors? This is apparently because funding for the monument ran out during the build. When workers were able to continue with the project 25 years later, the original stones couldn't be matched.

HAPPY TRAVELS!

Made in United States
North Haven, CT
07 March 2025